Soccer Session Planner Notebook

A Simple Way to Track Your Soccer Coaching Sessions

Chest Dugger

ABOUT THE AUTHOR

Chest Dugger is a pen name for our soccer coaching brand, Abiprod. We provide high quality soccer coaching tips, drills, fitness and mentality tips to ensure your success.

We have been fans of the beautiful game for decades. Like every soccer fan around the globe, we watch and play the beautiful game as much as we can. Whether we're fans of Manchester United, Real Madrid, Arsenal or LA Galaxy; we share a common love for the beautiful game.

Through our experiences, we've noticed that there's very little information for the common soccer fan who wants to escalate his game to the next level. Or get their kids started on the way. Too much of the information on the web and outside is too basic.

Being passionate about the game, we want to get the message across to as many people as possible. Through our soccer coaching blog, books and products; we aim to bring high quality soccer coaching to the world. Anyone who's passionate about the beautiful game can use our tactics and strategies. Here's a link to our author page for other books.

https://www.amazon.com/Chest-Dugger/e/B078L131DT/ref=sr_ntt_srch_lnk_1?qid=1514547441&sr=1-1

How To Use This Notebook

Be completely clear on the aim of the session. (this might be a part of a long-term development plan, or the response to assessment of a recent game or training session). Note: the aim does not need to be the same for every player. In fact, usually it should not be, since all players have different strengths and weaknesses.
Keep the principal aims down to two or three max per player. More than this, and the session becomes unfocussed.
The aims should be documented to help form a coherent plan over the season.

Paperwork should be kept to an absolute minimum. Soccer is a fluid, active sport. Have a simple grid for each session and match. Players down one side, key skills along the top. (one is attached). Complete it as you go along, or get a colleague to do so, and then finish off at the end. Never more than ten minutes. This should form the basis for future plans.

Date and Time:

Player	Stamina	Mental Fitness	First Touch	Heading	Off the Ball Movement	Dribbling	Shooting	Passing	Note

Notes:

Date and Time:

Player	Stamina	Mental Fitness	First Touch	Heading	Off the Ball Movement	Dribbling	Shooting	Passing	Note

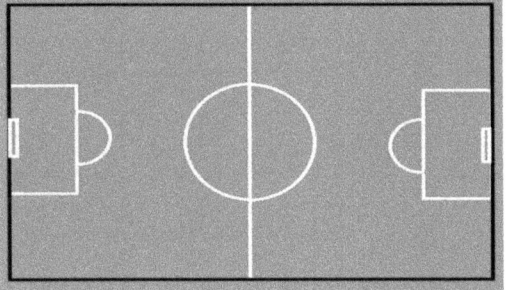

Notes:

Date and Time:

Player	Stamina	Mental Fitness	First Touch	Heading	Off the Ball Movement	Dribbling	Shooting	Passing	Note

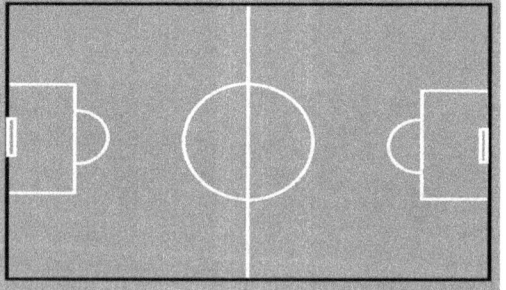

Notes:

Date and Time:

Player	Stamina	Mental Fitness	First Touch	Heading	Off the Ball Movement	Dribbling	Shooting	Passing	Note

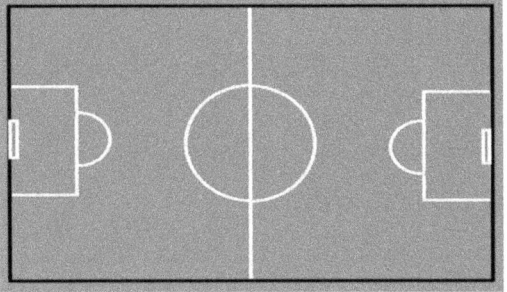

Notes:

Date and Time:

Note	Passing	Shooting	Dribbling	Off the Ball Movement	Heading	First Touch	Mental Fitness	Stamina	Player

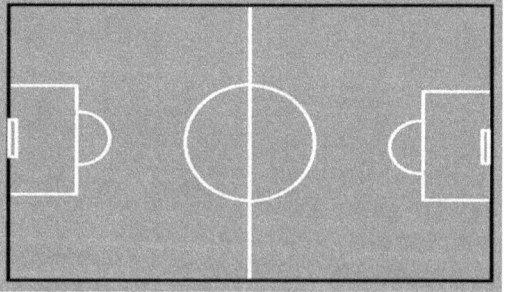

Notes:

Date and Time:

Player	Stamina	Mental Fitness	First Touch	Heading	Off the Ball Movement	Dribbling	Shooting	Passing	Note

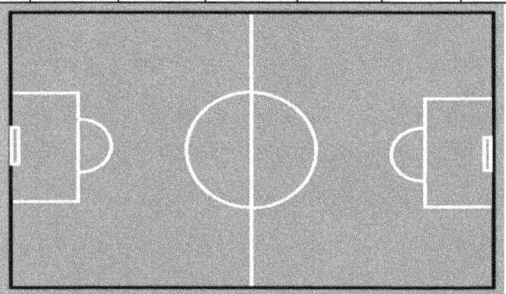

Notes:

Date and Time:

Note	Passing	Shooting	Dribbling	Off the Ball Movement	Heading	First Touch	Mental Fitness	Stamina	Player

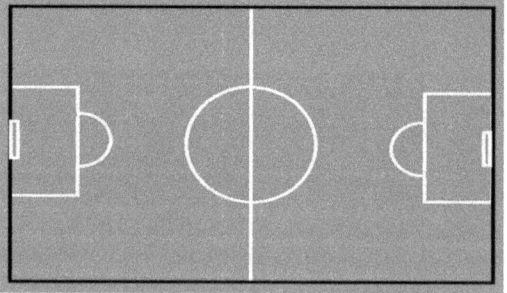

Notes:

Date and Time:

Player	Stamina	Mental Fitness	First Touch	Heading	Off the Ball Movement	Dribbling	Shooting	Passing	Note

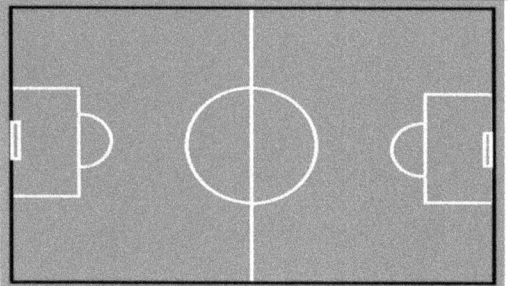

Notes:

Date and Time:

Player	Stamina	Mental Fitness	First Touch	Heading	Off the Ball Movement	Dribbling	Shooting	Passing	Note

Notes:

Date and Time:

Note	Passing	Shooting	Dribbling	Off the Ball Movement	Heading	First Touch	Mental Fitness	Stamina	Player

Notes:

Date and Time:

Player	Stamina	Mental Fitness	First Touch	Heading	Off the Ball Movement	Dribbling	Shooting	Passing	Note

Notes:

Date and Time:

Note	Passing	Shooting	Dribbling	Off the Ball Movement	Heading	First Touch	Mental Fitness	Stamina	Player

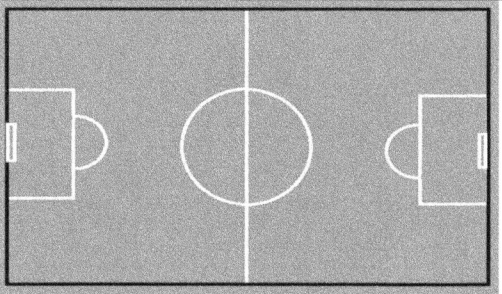

Notes:

Date and Time:

Note	Passing	Shooting	Dribbling	Off the Ball Movement	Heading	First Touch	Mental Fitness	Stamina	Player

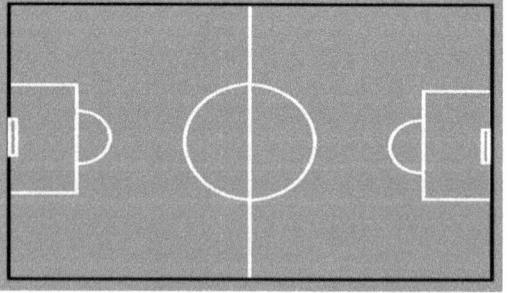

Notes:

Date and Time:

Note	Passing	Shooting	Dribbling	Off the Ball Movement	Heading	First Touch	Mental Fitness	Stamina	Player

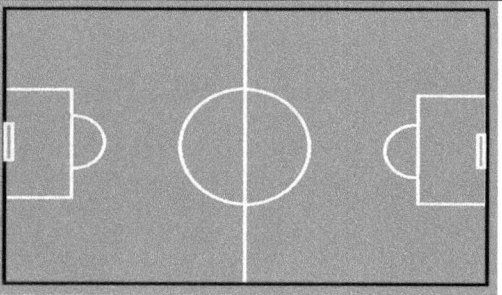

Notes:

Date and Time:

Player	Stamina	Mental Fitness	First Touch	Heading	Off the Ball Movement	Dribbling	Shooting	Passing	Note

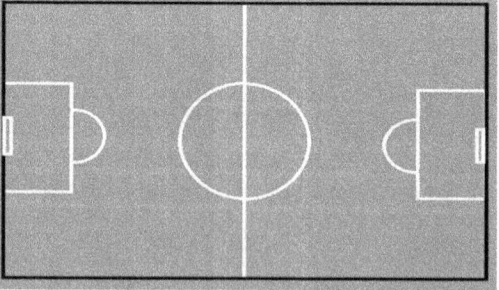

Notes:

Date and Time:

Player	Stamina	Mental Fitness	First Touch	Heading	Off the Ball Movement	Dribbling	Shooting	Passing	Note

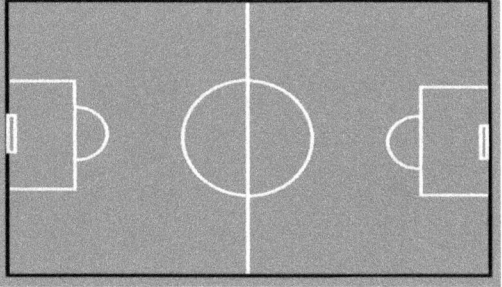

Notes:

Date and Time:

Note	Passing	Shooting	Dribbling	Off the Ball Movement	Heading	First Touch	Mental Fitness	Stamina	Player

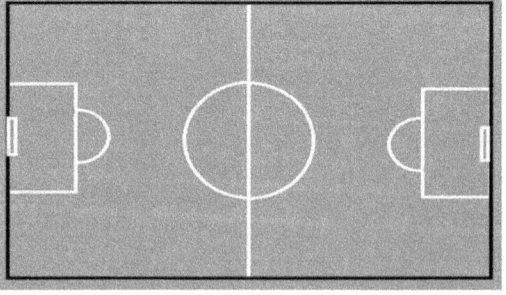

Notes:

Date and Time:

Note	Passing	Shooting	Dribbling	Off the Ball Movement	Heading	First Touch	Mental Fitness	Stamina	Player

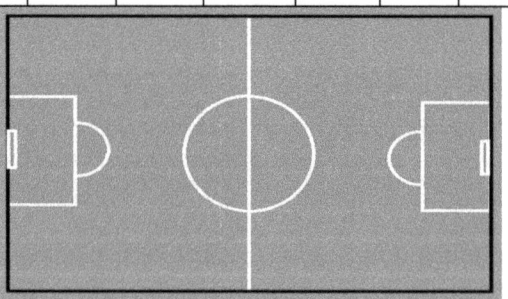

Notes:

Date and Time:

Note	Passing	Shooting	Dribbling	Off the Ball Movement	Heading	First Touch	Mental Fitness	Stamina	Player

Notes:

Date and Time:

Note	Passing	Shooting	Dribbling	Off the Ball Movement	Heading	First Touch	Mental Fitness	Stamina	Player

Notes:

Date and Time:

Player	Stamina	Mental Fitness	First Touch	Heading	Off the Ball Movement	Dribbling	Shooting	Passing	Note

Notes:

Date and Time:

Player	Stamina	Mental Fitness	First Touch	Heading	Off the Ball Movement	Dribbling	Shooting	Passing	Note

Notes:

Date and Time:

Note	Passing	Shooting	Dribbling	Off the Ball Movement	Heading	First Touch	Mental Fitness	Stamina	Player

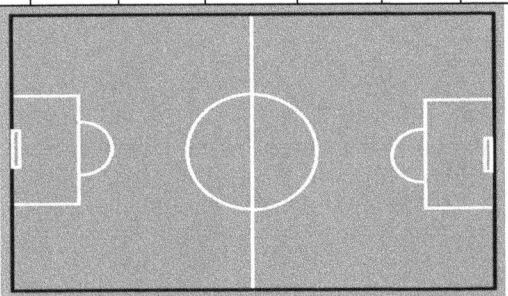

Notes:

Date and Time:

Player	Stamina	Mental Fitness	First Touch	Heading	Off the Ball Movement	Dribbling	Shooting	Passing	Note

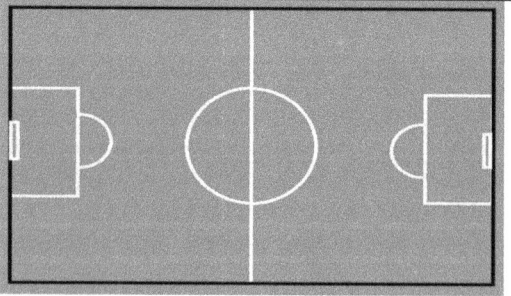

Notes:

Date and Time:

Player	Stamina	Mental Fitness	First Touch	Heading	Off the Ball Movement	Dribbling	Shooting	Passing	Note

Notes:

Date and Time:

Note	Passing	Shooting	Dribbling	Off the Ball Movement	Heading	First Touch	Mental Fitness	Stamina	Player

Notes:

Date and Time:

Note	Passing	Shooting	Dribbling	Off the Ball Movement	Heading	First Touch	Mental Fitness	Stamina	Player

Notes:

Date and Time:

Note	Passing	Shooting	Dribbling	Off the Ball Movement	Heading	First Touch	Mental Fitness	Stamina	Player

Notes:

Date and Time:

Player	Stamina	Mental Fitness	First Touch	Heading	Off the Ball Movement	Dribbling	Shooting	Passing	Note

Notes:

Date and Time:

Note	Passing	Shooting	Dribbling	Off the Ball Movement	Heading	First Touch	Mental Fitness	Stamina	Player

Notes:

Date and Time:

Player	Stamina	Mental Fitness	First Touch	Heading	Off the Ball Movement	Dribbling	Shooting	Passing	Note

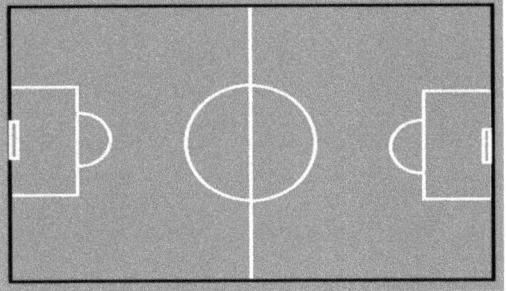

Notes:

Date and Time:

Note	Passing	Shooting	Dribbling	Off the Ball Movement	Heading	First Touch	Mental Fitness	Stamina	Player

Notes:

Date and Time:

Player	Stamina	Mental Fitness	First Touch	Heading	Off the Ball Movement	Dribbling	Shooting	Passing	Note

Notes:

Date and Time:

Note	Passing	Shooting	Dribbling	Off the Ball Movement	Heading	First Touch	Mental Fitness	Stamina	Player

Notes:

Date and Time:

Note	Passing	Shooting	Dribbling	Off the Ball Movement	Heading	First Touch	Mental Fitness	Stamina	Player

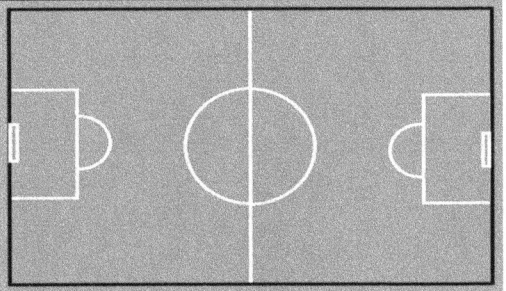

Notes:

Date and Time:

Player	Stamina	Mental Fitness	First Touch	Heading	Off the Ball Movement	Dribbling	Shooting	Passing	Note

Notes:

Date and Time:

Note	Passing	Shooting	Dribbling	Off the Ball Movement	Heading	First Touch	Mental Fitness	Stamina	Player

Notes:

Date and Time:

Player	Stamina	Mental Fitness	First Touch	Heading	Off the Ball Movement	Dribbling	Shooting	Passing	Note

Notes:

Date and Time:

Note	Passing	Shooting	Dribbling	Off the Ball Movement	Heading	First Touch	Mental Fitness	Stamina	Player

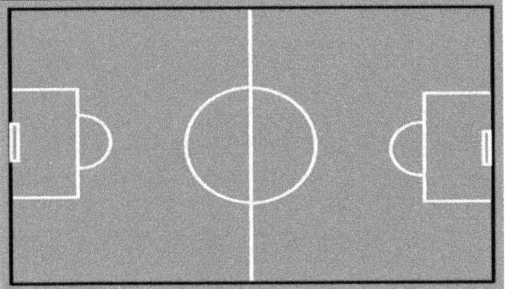

Notes:

Date and Time:

Player	Stamina	Mental Fitness	First Touch	Heading	Off the Ball Movement	Dribbling	Shooting	Passing	Note

Notes:

Date and Time:

Note	Passing	Shooting	Dribbling	Off the Ball Movement	Heading	First Touch	Mental Fitness	Stamina	Player

Notes:

Date and Time:

Player	Stamina	Mental Fitness	First Touch	Heading	Off the Ball Movement	Dribbling	Shooting	Passing	Note

Notes:

Date and Time:

Player	Stamina	Mental Fitness	First Touch	Heading	Off the Ball Movement	Dribbling	Shooting	Passing	Note

Notes:

Date and Time:

Note	Passing	Shooting	Dribbling	Off the Ball Movement	Heading	First Touch	Mental Fitness	Stamina	Player

Notes:

Date and Time:

Player	Stamina	Mental Fitness	First Touch	Heading	Off the Ball Movement	Dribbling	Shooting	Passing	Note

Notes:

Date and Time:

Player	Stamina	Mental Fitness	First Touch	Heading	Off the Ball Movement	Dribbling	Shooting	Passing	Note

Notes:

Date and Time:

Note	Passing	Shooting	Dribbling	Off the Ball Movement	Heading	First Touch	Mental Fitness	Stamina	Player

Notes:

Date and Time:

Note	Passing	Shooting	Dribbling	Off the Ball Movement	Heading	First Touch	Mental Fitness	Stamina	Player

Notes:

Date and Time:

Player	Stamina	Mental Fitness	First Touch	Heading	Off the Ball Movement	Dribbling	Shooting	Passing	Note

Notes:

Date and Time:

Player	Stamina	Mental Fitness	First Touch	Heading	Off the Ball Movement	Dribbling	Shooting	Passing	Note

Notes:

Date and Time:

Player	Stamina	Mental Fitness	First Touch	Heading	Off the Ball Movement	Dribbling	Shooting	Passing	Note

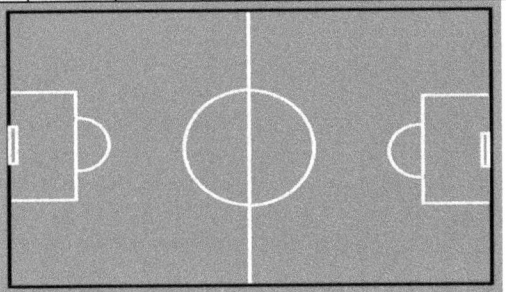

Notes:

Date and Time:

Player	Stamina	Mental Fitness	First Touch	Heading	Off the Ball Movement	Dribbling	Shooting	Passing	Note

Notes:

Date and Time:

Player	Stamina	Mental Fitness	First Touch	Heading	Off the Ball Movement	Dribbling	Shooting	Passing	Note

Notes:

Date and Time:

Player	Stamina	Mental Fitness	First Touch	Heading	Off the Ball Movement	Dribbling	Shooting	Passing	Note

Notes:

Date and Time:

Note	Passing	Shooting	Dribbling	Off the Ball Movement	Heading	First Touch	Mental Fitness	Stamina	Player

Notes:

Date and Time:

Player	Stamina	Mental Fitness	First Touch	Heading	Off the Ball Movement	Dribbling	Shooting	Passing	Note

Notes:

Date and Time:

Note	Passing	Shooting	Dribbling	Off the Ball Movement	Heading	First Touch	Mental Fitness	Stamina	Player

Notes:

Date and Time:

Player	Stamina	Mental Fitness	First Touch	Heading	Off the Ball Movement	Dribbling	Shooting	Passing	Note

Notes:

Date and Time:

Player	Stamina	Mental Fitness	First Touch	Heading	Off the Ball Movement	Dribbling	Shooting	Passing	Note

Notes:

Date and Time:

Player	Stamina	Mental Fitness	First Touch	Heading	Off the Ball Movement	Dribbling	Shooting	Passing	Note

Notes:

Date and Time:

Note	Passing	Shooting	Dribbling	Off the Ball Movement	Heading	First Touch	Mental Fitness	Stamina	Player

Notes:

Date and Time:

Note	Passing	Shooting	Dribbling	Off the Ball Movement	Heading	First Touch	Mental Fitness	Stamina	Player

Notes:

Date and Time:

Note	Passing	Shooting	Dribbling	Off the Ball Movement	Heading	First Touch	Mental Fitness	Stamina	Player

Notes:

Date and Time:

Player	Stamina	Mental Fitness	First Touch	Heading	Off the Ball Movement	Dribbling	Shooting	Passing	Note

Notes:

Date and Time:

Note	Passing	Shooting	Dribbling	Off the Ball Movement	Heading	First Touch	Mental	Fitness	Stamina	Player

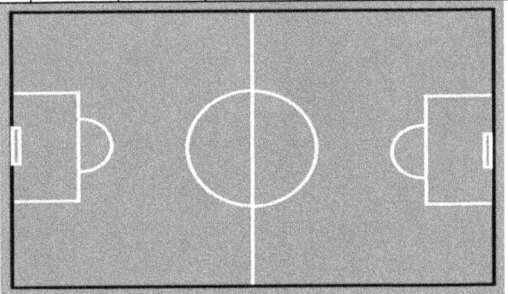

Notes:

Date and Time:

Player	Stamina	Mental Fitness	First Touch	Heading	Off the Ball Movement	Dribbling	Shooting	Passing	Note

Notes:

Date and Time:

Note	Passing	Shooting	Dribbling	Off the Ball Movement	Heading	First Touch	Mental Fitness	Stamina	Player

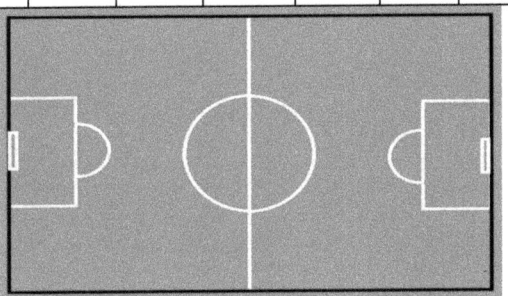

Notes:

Date and Time:

Player	Stamina	Mental Fitness	First Touch	Heading	Off the Ball Movement	Dribbling	Shooting	Passing	Note

Notes:

Date and Time:

Note	Passing	Shooting	Dribbling	Off the Ball Movement	Heading	First Touch	Mental	Fitness	Stamina	Player

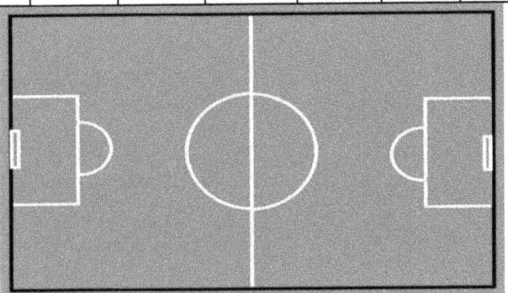

Notes:

Date and Time:

Note	Passing	Shooting	Dribbling	Off the Ball Movement	Heading	First Touch	Mental Fitness	Stamina	Player

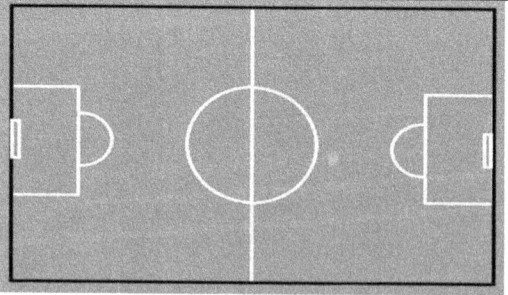

Notes:

Date and Time:

Note	Passing	Shooting	Dribbling	Off the Ball Movement	Heading	First Touch	Mental Fitness	Stamina	Player

Notes:

Date and Time:

Player	Stamina	Mental Fitness	First Touch	Heading	Off the Ball Movement	Dribbling	Shooting	Passing	Note

Notes:

Date and Time:

Player	Stamina	Mental Fitness	First Touch	Heading	Off the Ball Movement	Dribbling	Shooting	Passing	Note

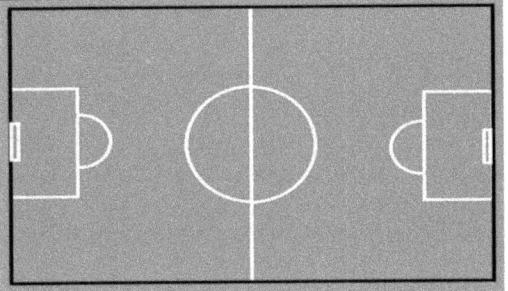

Notes:

Date and Time:

Note	Passing	Shooting	Dribbling	Off the Ball Movement	Heading	First Touch	Mental Fitness	Stamina	Player

Notes:

Date and Time:

Note	Passing	Shooting	Dribbling	Off the Ball Movement	Heading	First Touch	Mental Fitness	Stamina	Player

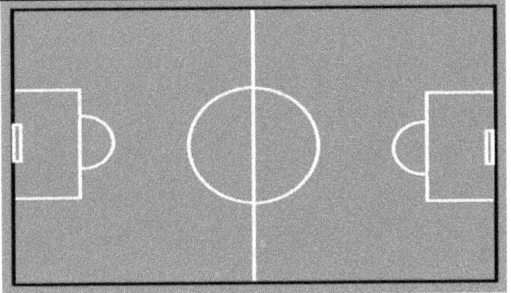

Notes:

Date and Time:

Player	Stamina	Mental Fitness	First Touch	Heading	Off the Ball Movement	Dribbling	Shooting	Passing	Note

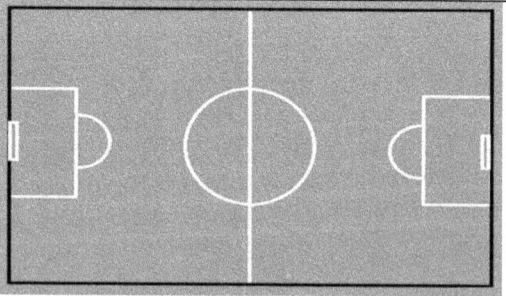

Notes:

Date and Time:

Note	Passing	Shooting	Dribbling	Off the Ball Movement	Heading	First Touch	Mental Fitness	Stamina	Player

Notes:

Date and Time:

Player	Stamina	Mental Fitness	First Touch	Heading	Off the Ball Movement	Dribbling	Shooting	Passing	Note

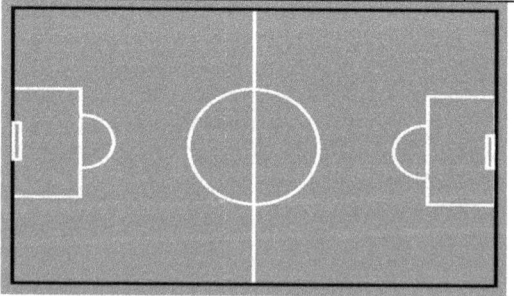

Notes:

Date and Time:

Note	Passing	Shooting	Dribbling	Off the Ball Movement	Heading	First Touch	Mental Fitness	Stamina	Player

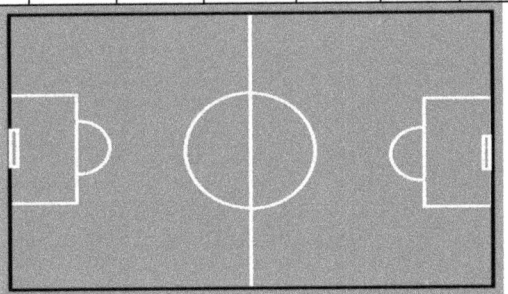

Notes:

Date and Time:

Player	Stamina	Mental Fitness	First Touch	Heading	Off the Ball Movement	Dribbling	Shooting	Passing	Note

Notes:

Date and Time:

Player	Stamina	Mental Fitness	First Touch	Heading	Off the Ball Movement	Dribbling	Shooting	Passing	Note

Notes:

Date and Time:

Player	Stamina	Mental Fitness	First Touch	Heading	Off the Ball Movement	Dribbling	Shooting	Passing	Note

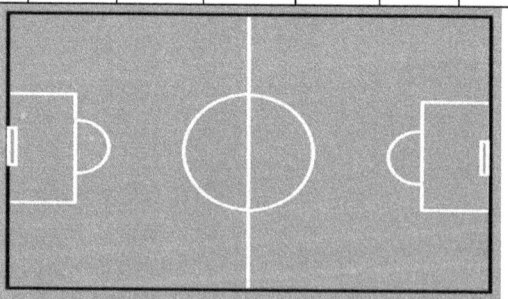

Notes:

Date and Time:

Note	Passing	Shooting	Dribbling	Off the Ball Movement	Heading	First Touch	Mental Fitness	Stamina	Player

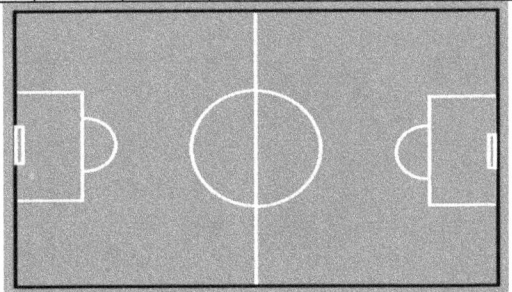

Notes:

Date and Time:

Note	Passing	Shooting	Dribbling	Off the Ball Movement	Heading	First Touch	Mental Fitness	Stamina	Player

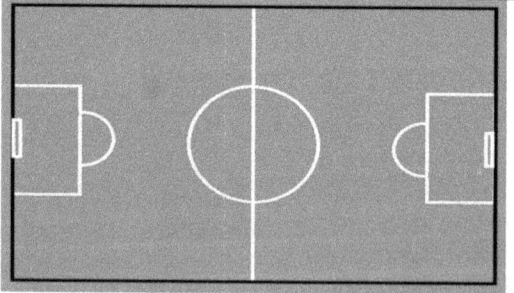

Notes:

Date and Time:

Player	Stamina	Mental Fitness	First Touch	Heading	Off the Ball Movement	Dribbling	Shooting	Passing	Note

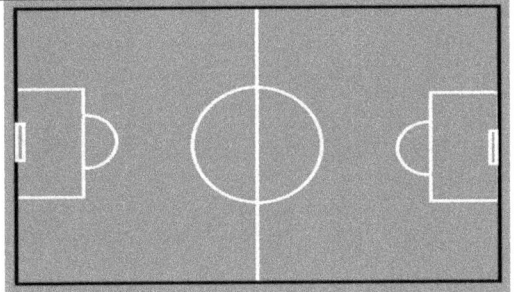

Notes:

Date and Time:

Player	Stamina	Mental Fitness	First Touch	Heading	Off the Ball Movement	Dribbling	Shooting	Passing	Note

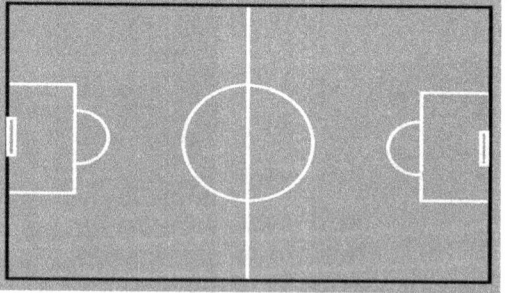

Notes:

Date and Time:

Player	Stamina	Mental Fitness	First Touch	Heading	Off the Ball Movement	Dribbling	Shooting	Passing	Note

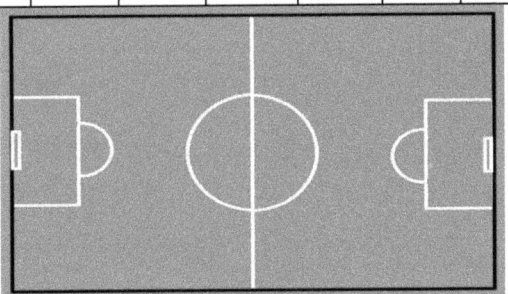

Notes:

Date and Time:

Player	Stamina	Mental Fitness	First Touch	Heading	Off the Ball Movement	Dribbling	Shooting	Passing	Note

Notes:

Date and Time:

Note	Passing	Shooting	Dribbling	Off the Ball Movement	Heading	First Touch	Mental Fitness	Stamina	Player

Notes:

Date and Time:

Player	Stamina	Mental Fitness	First Touch	Heading	Off the Ball Movement	Dribbling	Shooting	Passing	Note

Notes:

Date and Time:

Player	Stamina	Mental Fitness	First Touch	Heading	Off the Ball Movement	Dribbling	Shooting	Passing	Note

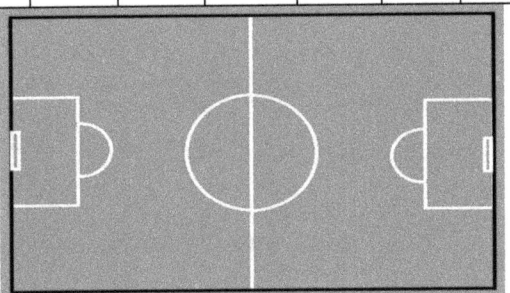

Notes:

Date and Time:

Player	Stamina	Mental Fitness	First Touch	Heading	Off the Ball Movement	Dribbling	Shooting	Passing	Note

Notes:

Date and Time:

Note	Passing	Shooting	Dribbling	Off the Ball Movement	Heading	First Touch	Mental Fitness	Stamina	Player

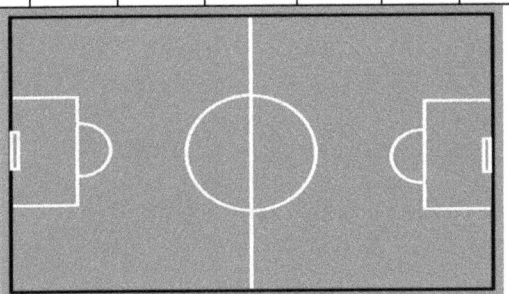

Notes:

Date and Time:

Player	Stamina	Mental Fitness	First Touch	Heading	Off the Ball Movement	Dribbling	Shooting	Passing	Note

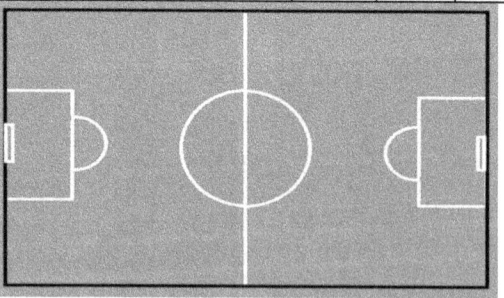

Notes:

Date and Time:

Player	Stamina	Mental Fitness	First Touch	Heading	Off the Ball Movement	Dribbling	Shooting	Passing	Note

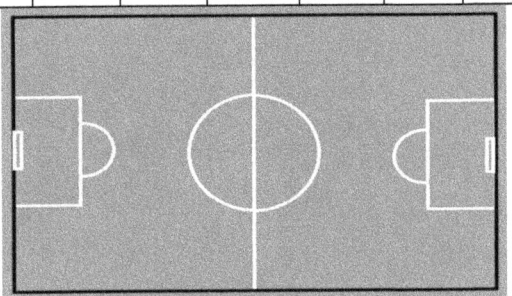

Notes:

Date and Time:

Note	Passing	Shooting	Dribbling	Off the Ball Movement	Heading	First Touch	Mental Fitness	Stamina	Player

Notes:

Date and Time:

Player	Stamina	Mental Fitness	First Touch	Heading	Off the Ball Movement	Dribbling	Shooting	Passing	Note

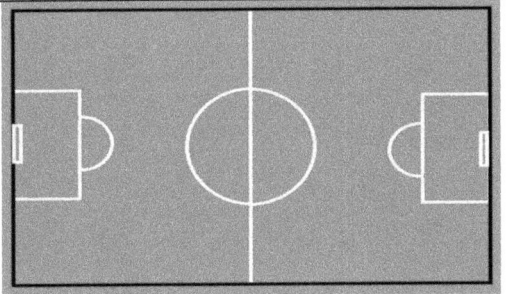

Notes:

Date and Time:

Note	Passing	Shooting	Dribbling	Off the Ball Movement	Heading	First Touch	Mental Fitness	Stamina	Player

Notes:

Date and Time:

Player	Stamina	Mental Fitness	First Touch	Heading	Off the Ball Movement	Dribbling	Shooting	Passing	Note

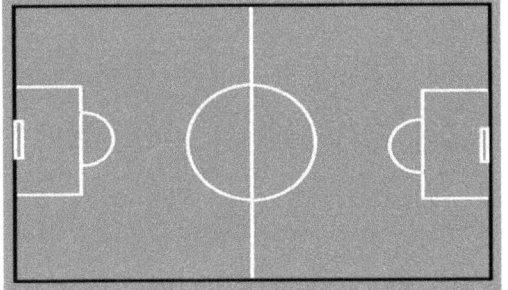

Notes:

Date and Time:

Note	Passing	Shooting	Dribbling	Off the Ball Movement	Heading	First Touch	Mental Fitness	Stamina	Player

Notes: